Mamma can do it .com

Unlocking Creativity | You can do it.

Germ Free Face Mask
Pattern & Tutorial

Germ Free Face Mask Pattern - Index

Germ Free Face Mask
Pattern & Tutorial

Supply List:
- Scrap Fabric - any type
  OR 1 pillowcase
  OR 1/4 yd muslin
- 1/8" elastic (20-24")

Fabric Choices on a Budget
The best type of fabric to use is whatever you have on hand! Use cotton quilting fabric from your scrap bin, an old t-shirt, a flannel shirt, a cloth napkin, curtains, muslin - the list goes on!

What type to make:
There are two types of face masks that you can sew with this pattern and tutorial. The FITTED face mask is very comfortable and doesn't creep up. However, it takes longer to make. The FAST face mask is VERY easy and fast. You'll have it done lickety split! It's comfortable too - Let me know which one you prefer and why!

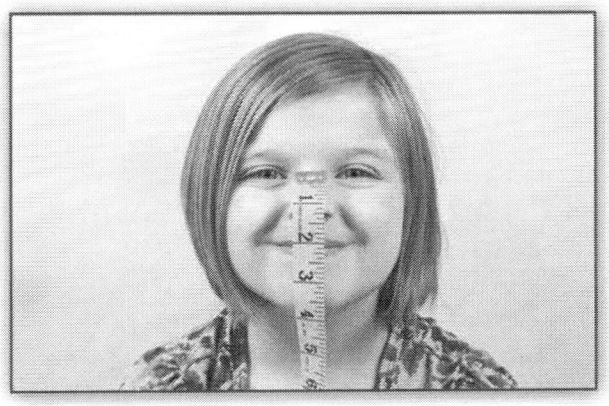

Determine what size to make your mask by measuring from between your eyes, to the bottom of your chin.
See the Size Chart on the pattern piece.

Fitted Face Mask Tutorial
See page 8 For the FAST Face Mask Tutorial

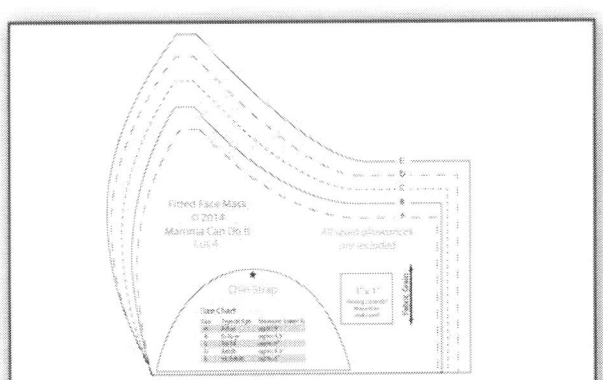

Step 1.
Print pattern piece.
Determine what size to make.

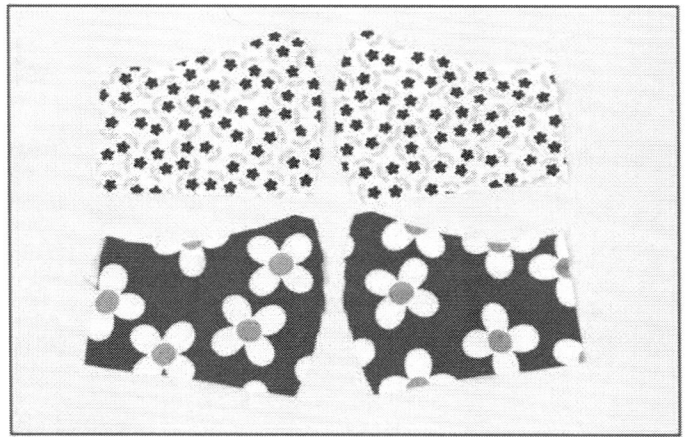

Step 2.
Use the pattern to cut 4.
There will be an INNER side and an OUTER side. When you cut, make the INNER fabrics mirror each other and the OUTER fabrics mirror each other.

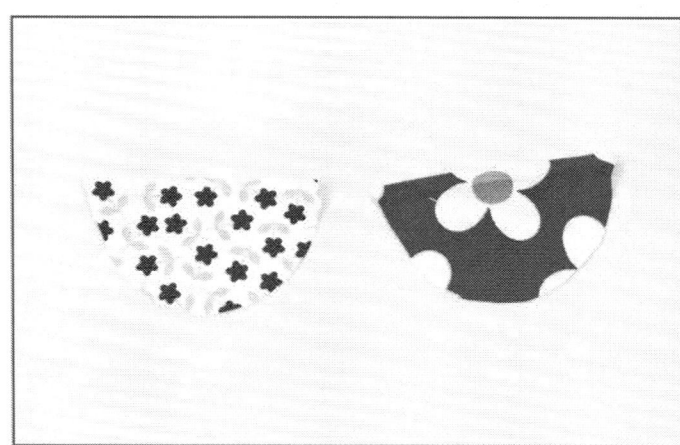

Step 3.
Use the *Chin Strap Pattern* piece to cut 2.
Set Aside.

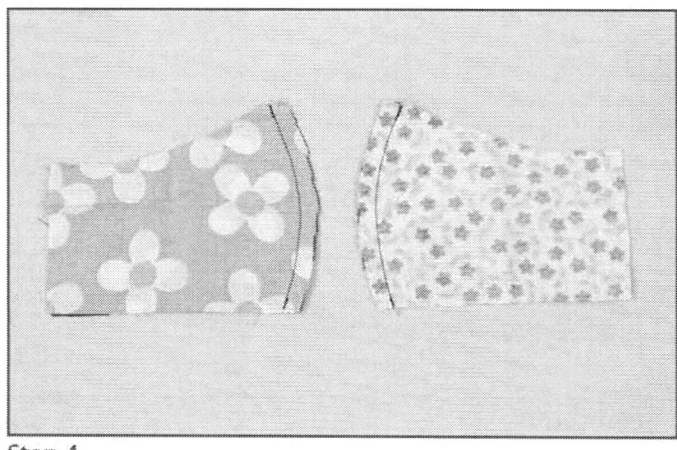

Step 4.
Place the mask pieces together with the *right sides* facing each other. *Put the INNER sides together and the OUTER sides together as shown.*
Sew 3/8" from the CURVED edge of each piece with a straight stitch.

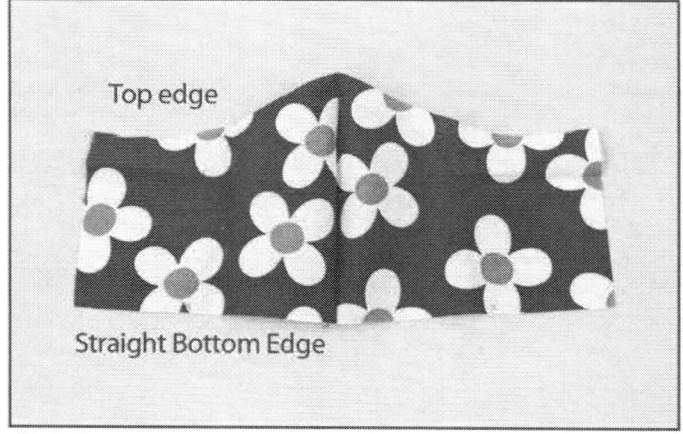

Step 5.
Open the mask pieces so that the *right side* is facing upward at you.

Step 6.
Locate the center of the curved edge on the matching chin strap. Mark with a pin.

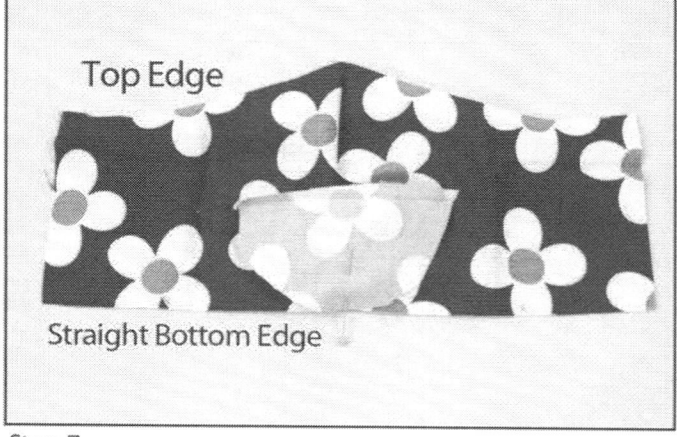

Step 7.
Place the chin strap with the *right side* facing down. Pin the center point of the chin strap directly onto the seam while lining up the straight bottom edge with the edge of the chin strap.

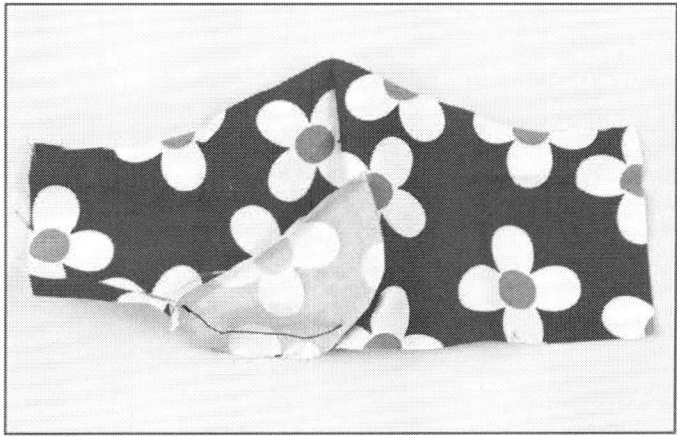

Step 8.
Starting at the center of the chin strap, slowly sew half of the curved edge of the chin strap onto the straight edge of the mask. Sew 3/8" from the edge with a straight stitch. *Take your time. It's worth it.*

Step 9.
Sew the remaining side of the chin strap.

Step 10.
Attach the remaining chin strap to the remaining mask pieces.

Step 11.
You should now have 2 mask pieces. Turn one mask piece with the *right side* facing downward. Turn the other mask piece with the *right side* facing upward.

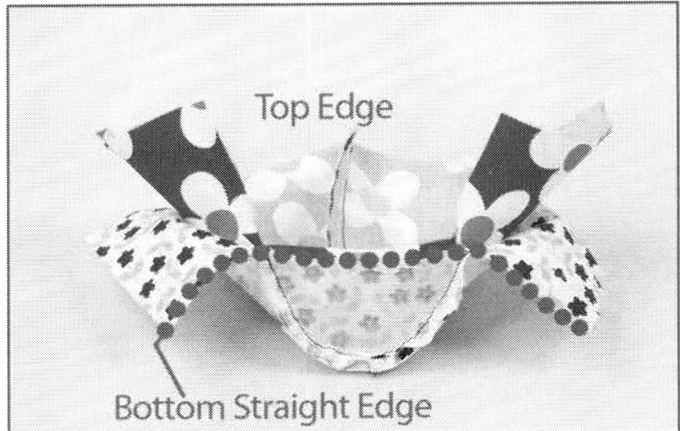

Top Edge

Bottom Straight Edge

Step 12.
Put the two pieces together with the *right sides* facing together. Line up the chin straps. Pin into place. *Don't skip the pinning.*

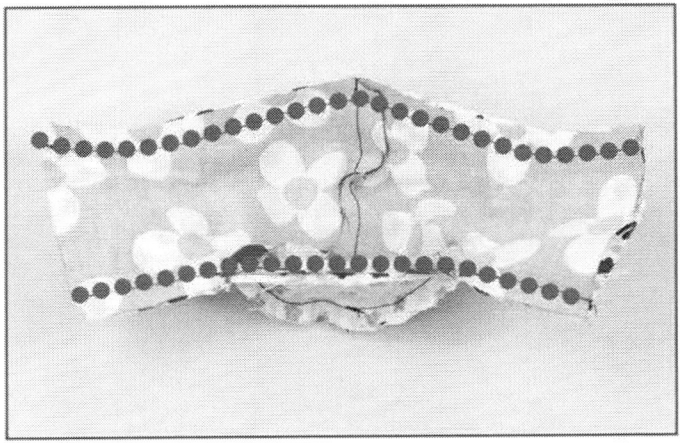

Step 13.
Sew the Bottom Straight edge and the top curved edge. Sew 3/8" from the edge with a straight stitch.

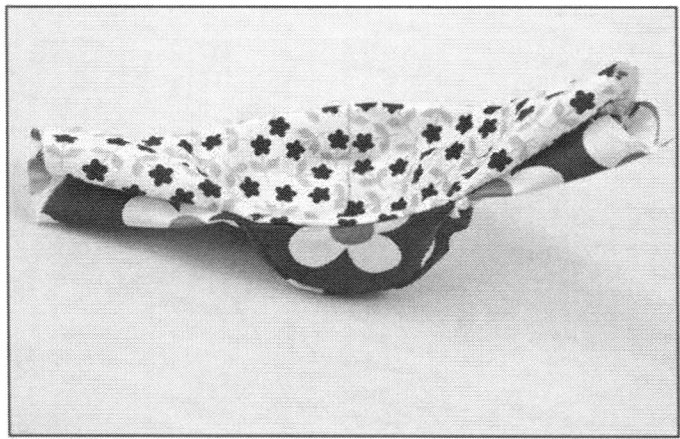

Step 14.
Turn the mask *right side out* through one of the open ends.

Step 15.
Fold each end inside of itself 1/2".
Iron the ends and edges of the mask flat.

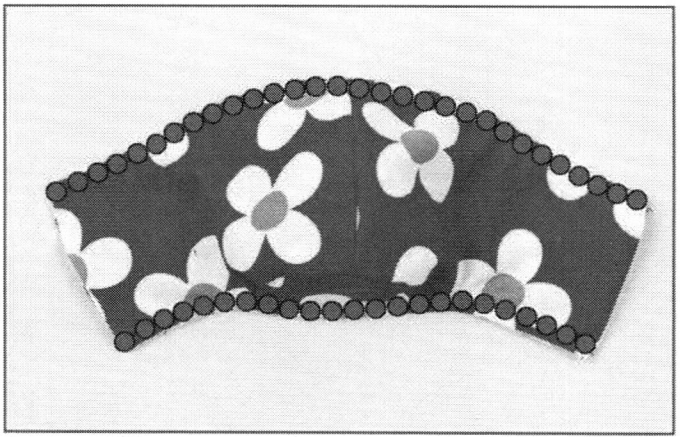

Step 16.
Top stitch the *top edge* and the *bottom edge*. To "top stitch", simply sew 1/8" from the edge with a straight stitch. *This creates a nice finish that will hold in place.*

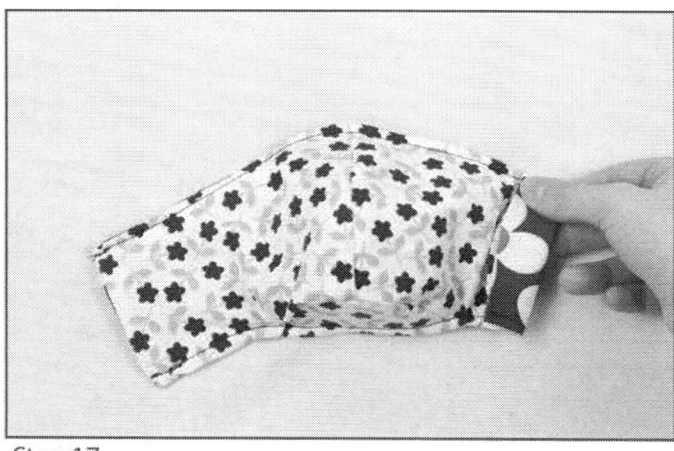

Step 17.
Determine which side you will want against your face. Place it facing upward. Fold the ends inward 3/4".

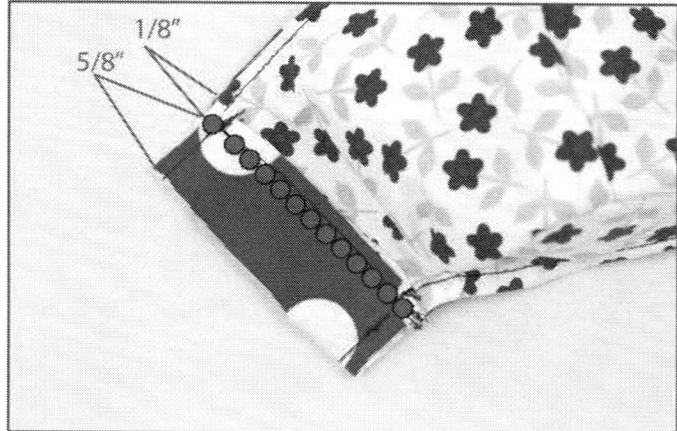

1/8"
5/8"

Step 18.
Sew the folded ends into place. Sew 1/8" from the inner edge of the fold (or 5/8" from the outer edge).

This creates a tube for elastic to thread through.
It also seals the openings on the ends.

Step 19.
Attach safety pins to 10" pieces of 1/8" elastic. Thread the safety pin through the tube from previous step.

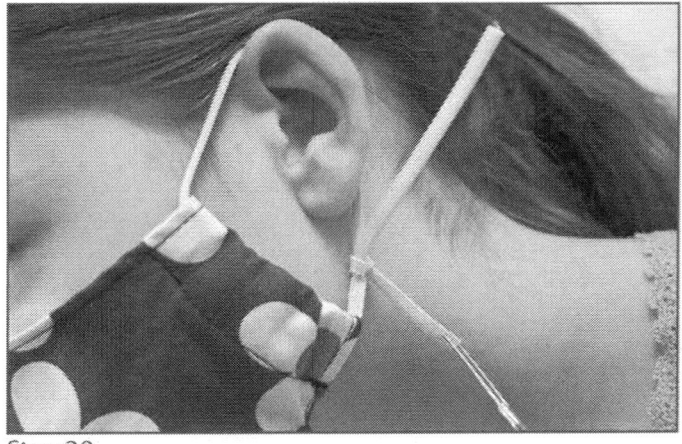

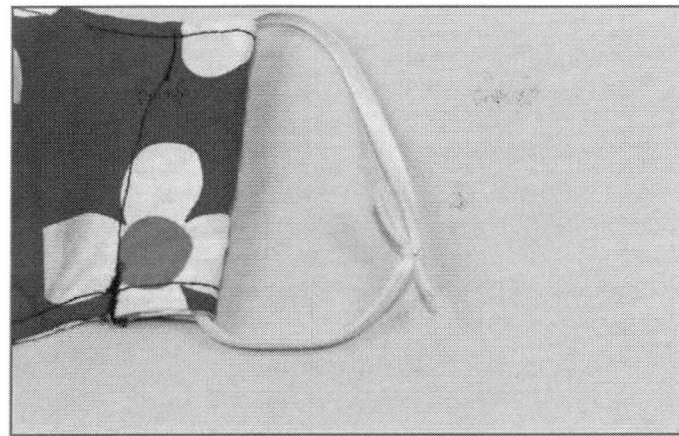

Step 20.
Place the mask on the wearer. Tie the elastic in a knot so that it fits the face comfortably.

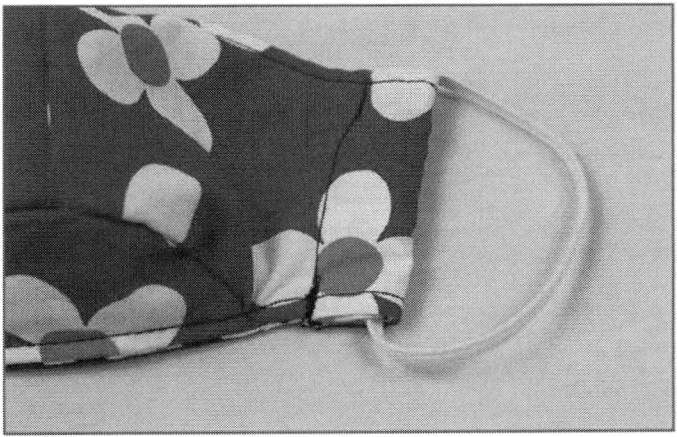

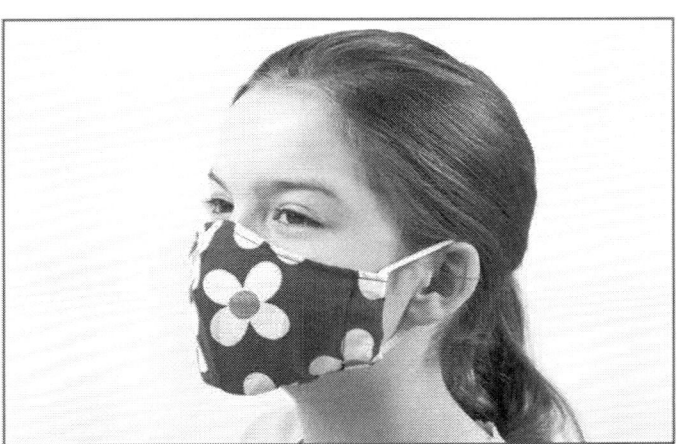

Step 21.
Turn the elastic so that the tied ends are hidden inside the tube.

Stay Germ Free!

FAST Face Mask Tutorial

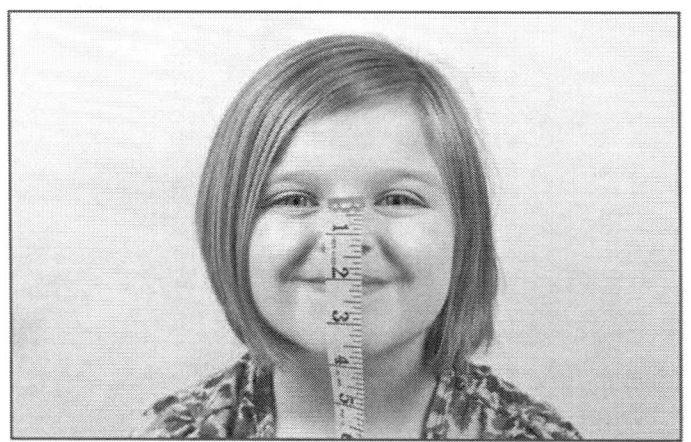

Determine what size to make your mask by measuring from between your eyes, to the bottom of your chin. See the Size Chart on the pattern piece.

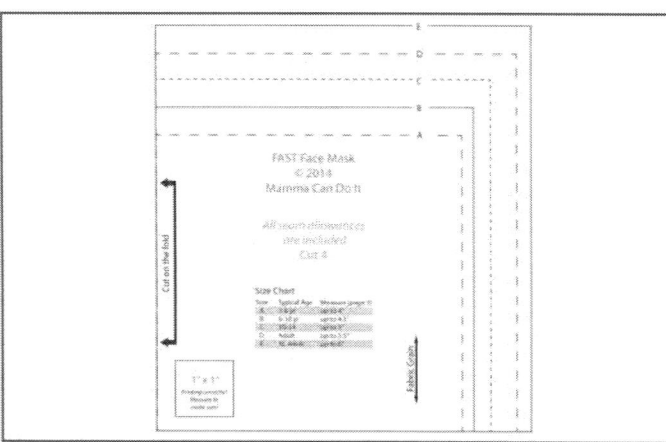

Step 22.
Print pattern piece and determine which size to make.

Step 23.
Cut 2 with the pattern piece.

Step 24.
Place the two pieces together with the *right sides* facing together.

Step 25.
Sew around all edges, but leave a 2" opening for turning *right side out.*

The opening should not be too close to the corner as it can cause issues with tucking it in later.

Step 26.
Clip off each corner. Be careful not to clip the seam that you just sewed.
This is important to help the mask's corners be flat and easy to sew through.

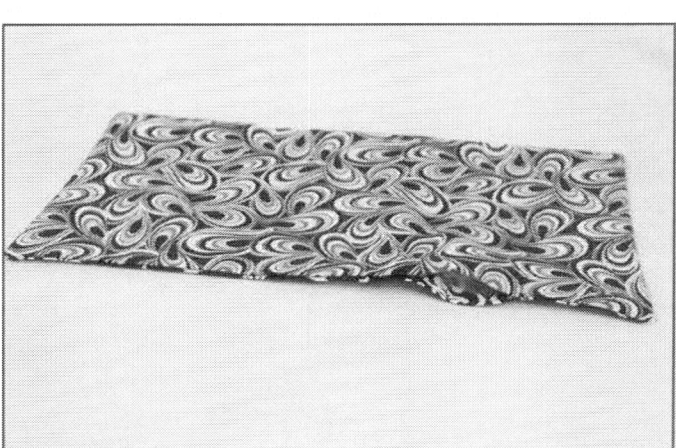

Step 27.
Turn *right side* out and iron flat.

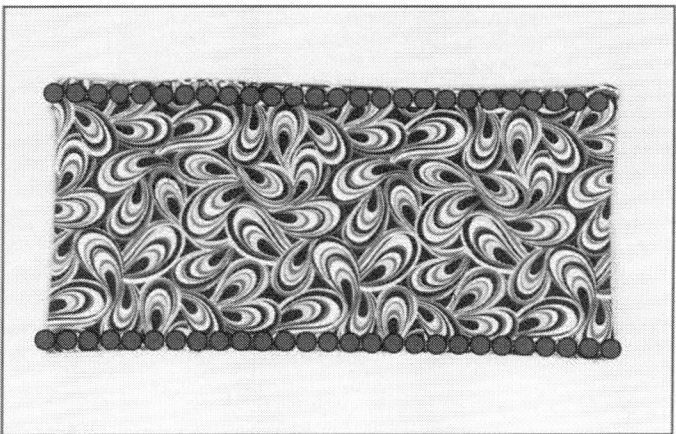

Step 28.
Sew a top stitch on each long edge.
A top stitch is a straight stitch that is about 1/8" from the edge.

Step 29.
Deternine which fabric will be against your face.
Fold over each short edge 3/4" toward the "face side".
In ths example, the green swirly fabric will be against my face.

5/8" 1/8"

Step 30.
Sew the folded ends into place. Sew 1/8" from the inner edge of the fold (or 5/8" from the outer.)

This creates a tube on each side of mask for elastic to go through.

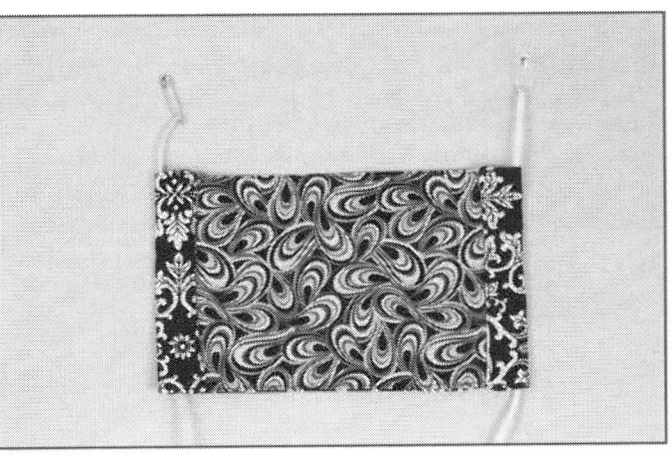

Step 31.
Attach 2, 12" long pieces of elastic to a safety pin. Fish the elastic through the elastic tube on each side of mask.

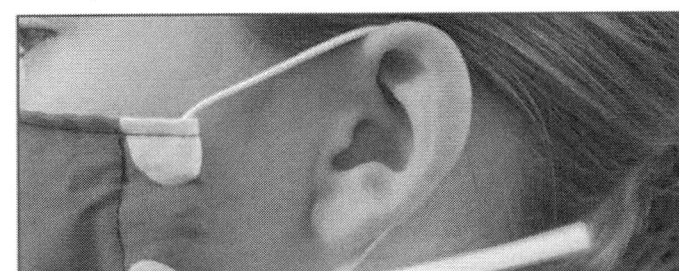

Step 32.
Try the mask on the wearer. Tie the elastic to fit.

Step 33.
Turn the elastic so that the tied ends are hiden inside the tube.

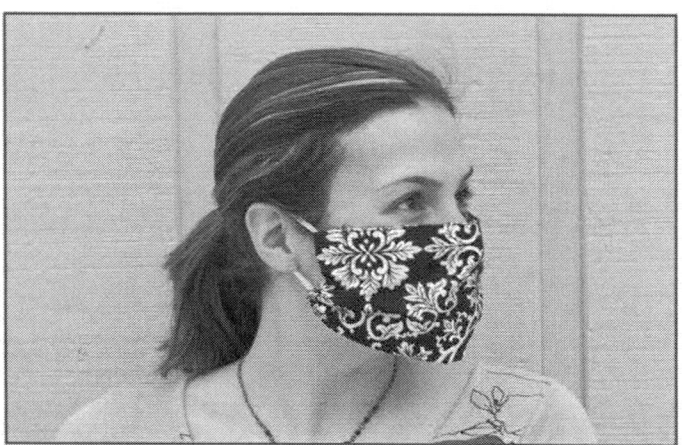

Stay Germ Free!

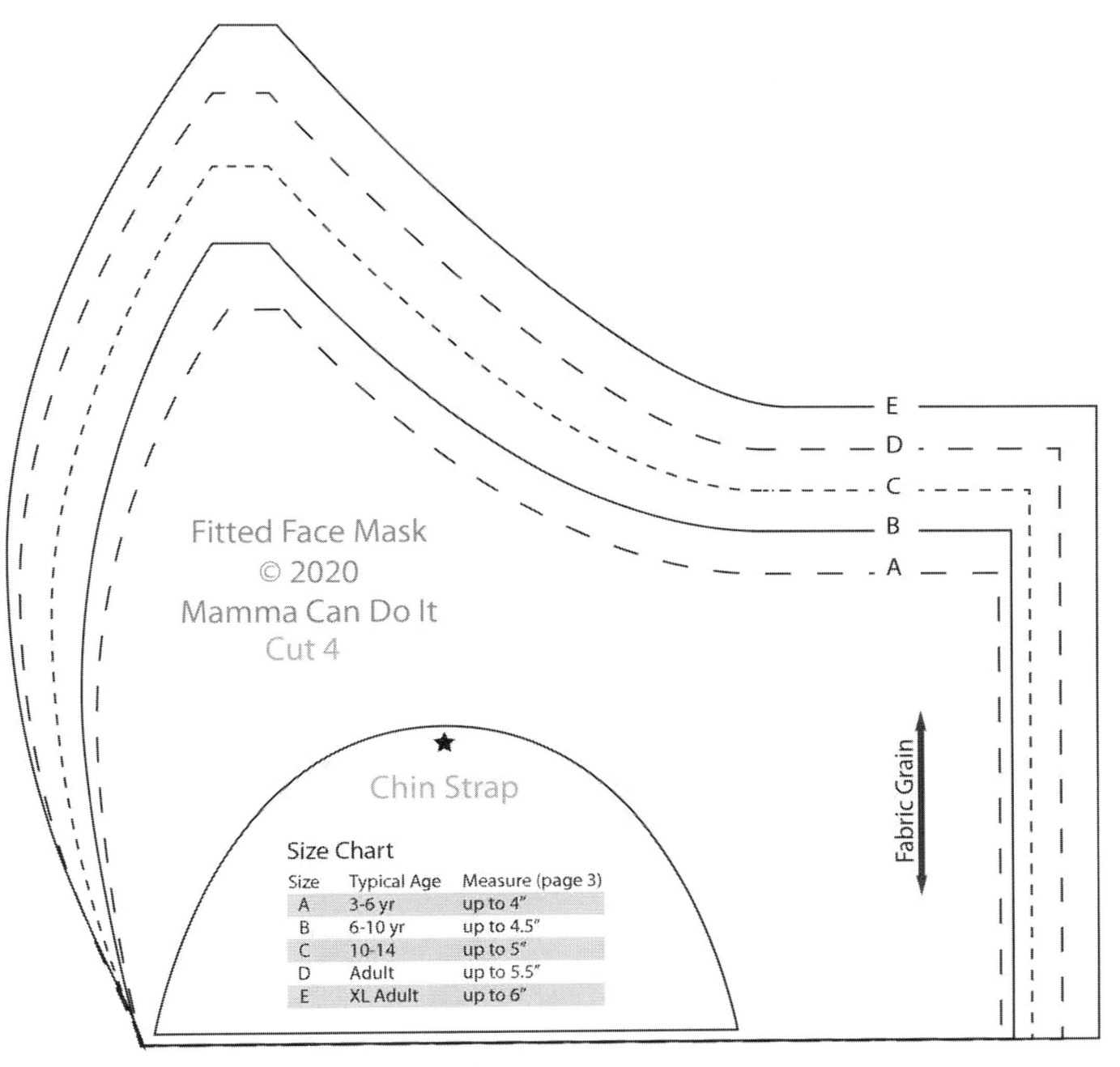

Fitted Face Mask
© 2020
Mamma Can Do It
Cut 4

Chin Strap

E
D
C
B
A

Fabric Grain

Size Chart

Size	Typical Age	Measure (page 3)
A	3-6 yr	up to 4"
B	6-10 yr	up to 4.5"
C	10-14	up to 5"
D	Adult	up to 5.5"
E	XL Adult	up to 6"

This page is intentionally blank

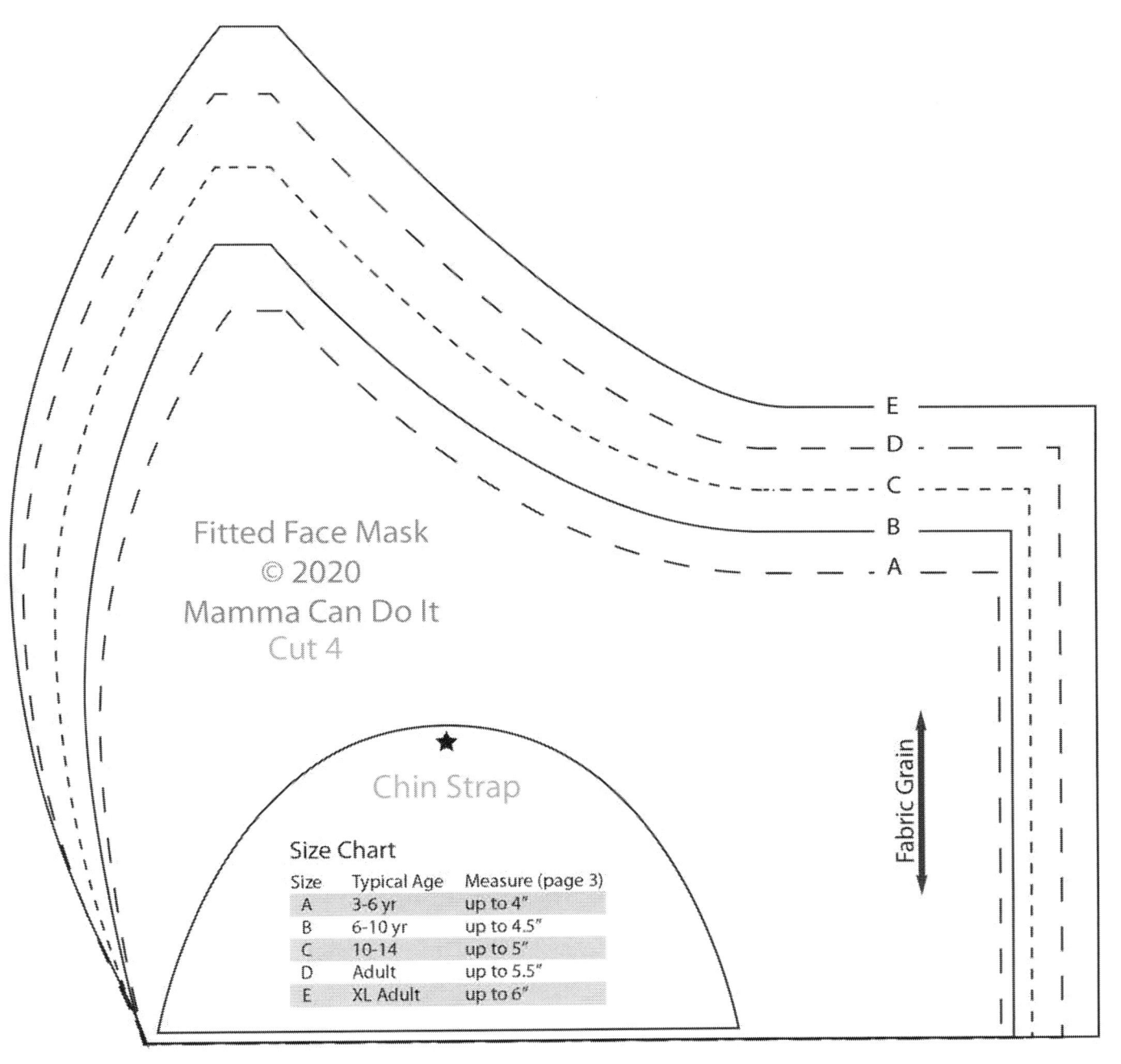

Fitted Face Mask
© 2020
Mamma Can Do It
Cut 4

Chin Strap

E
D
C
B
A

Fabric Grain

Size Chart

Size	Typical Age	Measure (page 3)
A	3-6 yr	up to 4"
B	6-10 yr	up to 4.5"
C	10-14	up to 5"
D	Adult	up to 5.5"
E	XL Adult	up to 6"

This page is intentionally blank

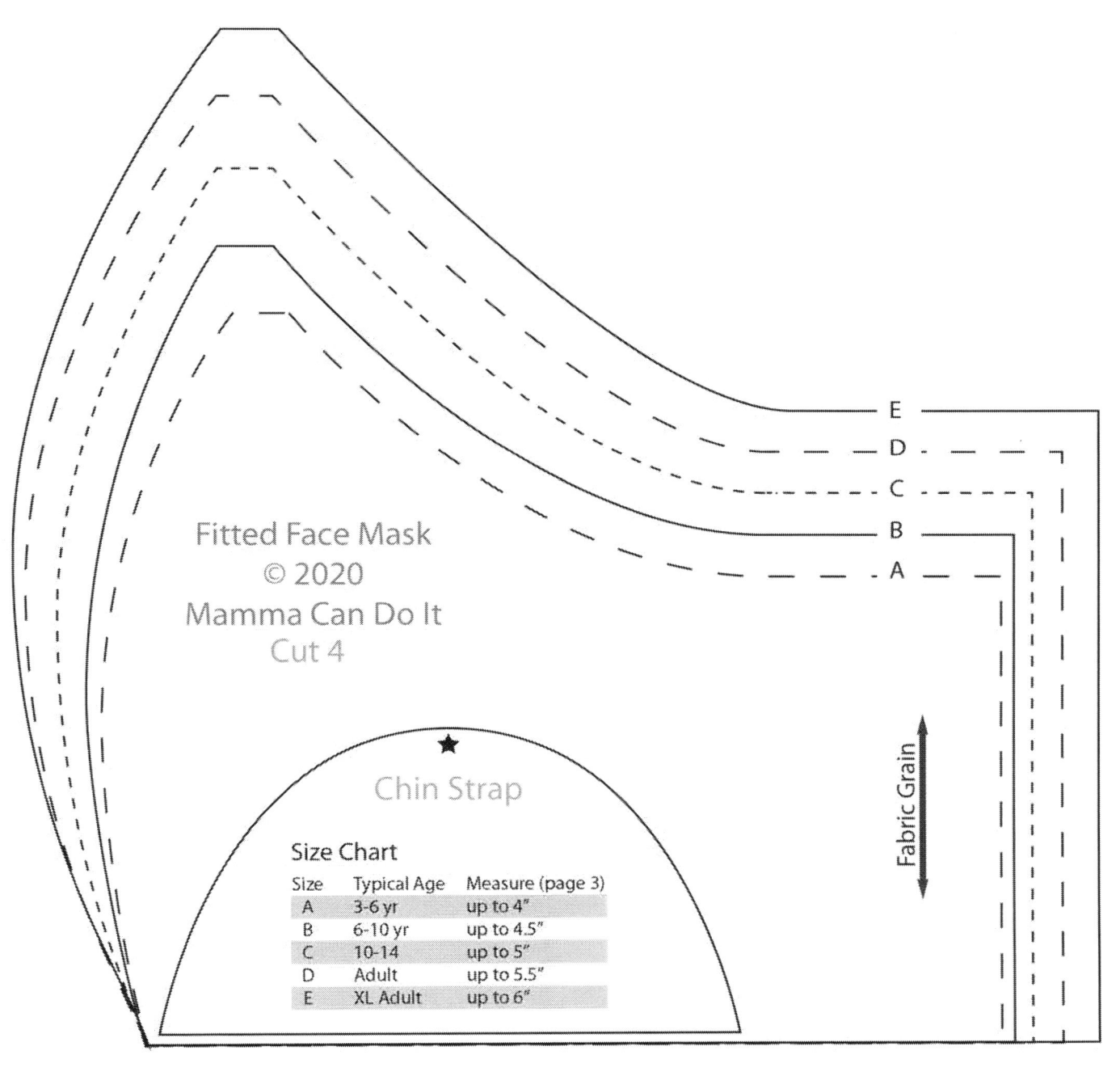

Fitted Face Mask
© 2020
Mamma Can Do It
Cut 4

Chin Strap

E
D
C
B
A

Fabric Grain

Size Chart

Size	Typical Age	Measure (page 3)
A	3-6 yr	up to 4"
B	6-10 yr	up to 4.5"
C	10-14	up to 5"
D	Adult	up to 5.5"
E	XL Adult	up to 6"

This page is intentionally blank

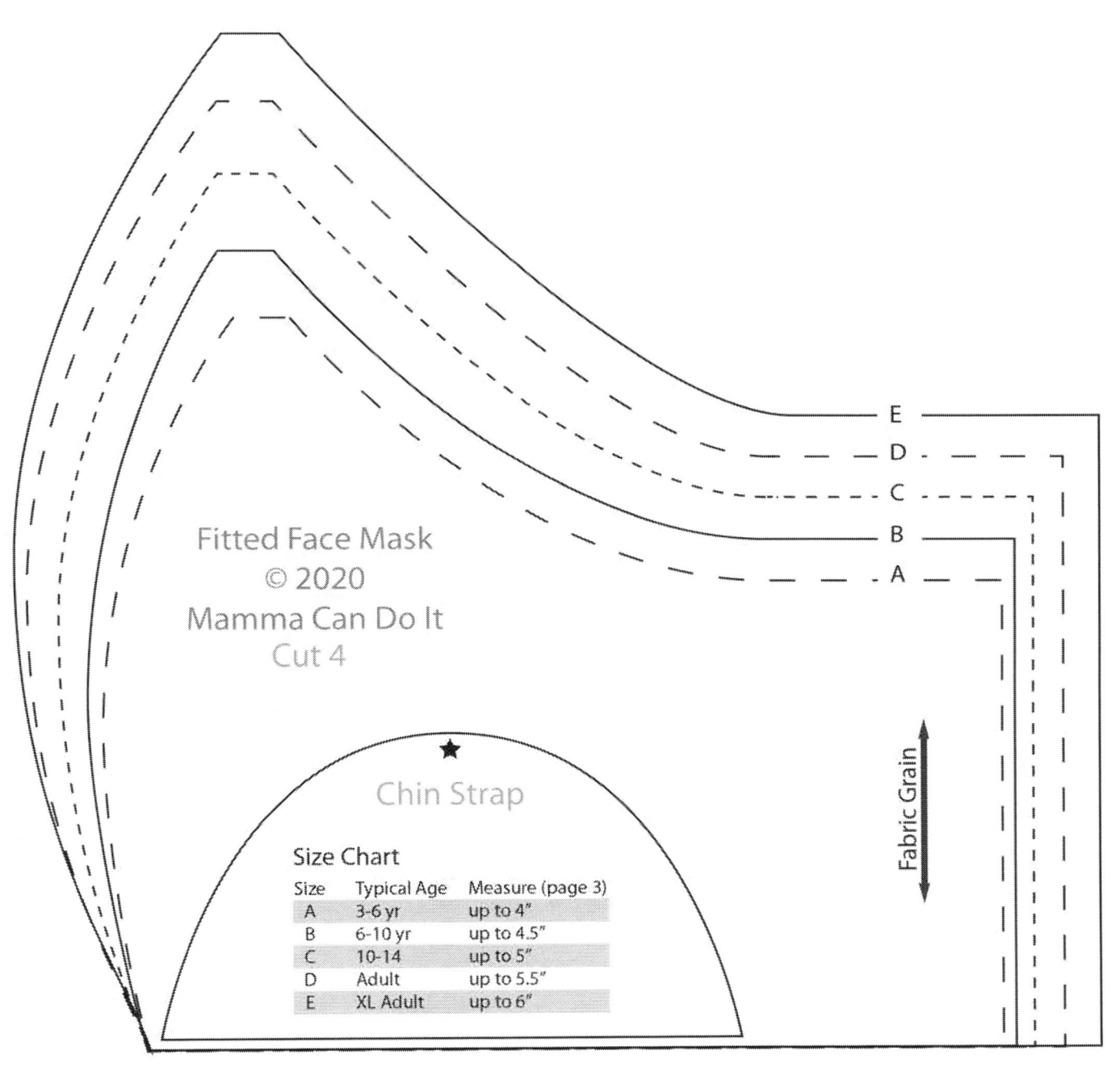

Fitted Face Mask
© 2020
Mamma Can Do It
Cut 4

E
D
C
B
A

Fabric Grain

Chin Strap

Size Chart

Size	Typical Age	Measure (page 3)
A	3-6 yr	up to 4"
B	6-10 yr	up to 4.5"
C	10-14	up to 5"
D	Adult	up to 5.5"
E	XL Adult	up to 6"

This page is intentionally blank

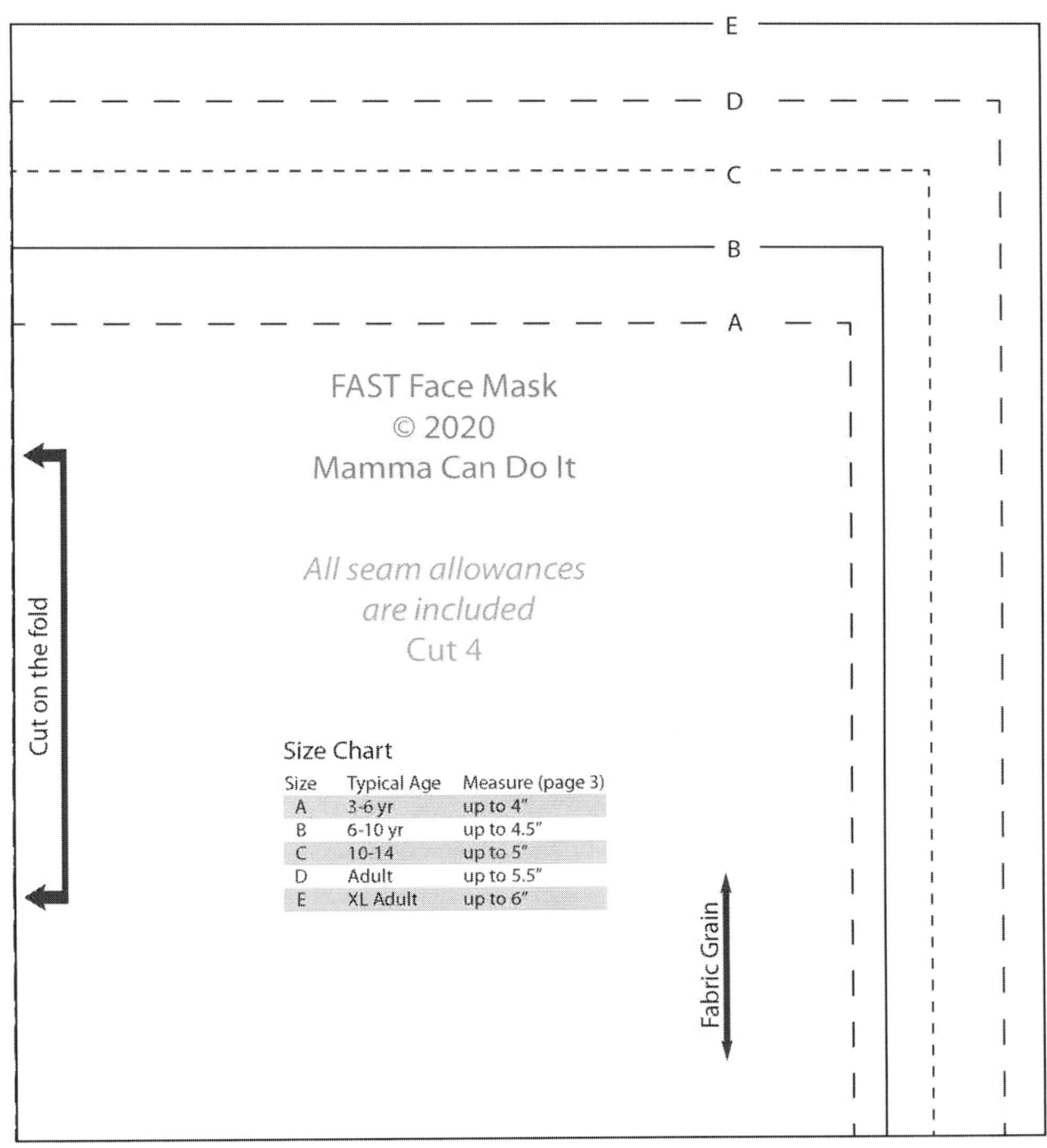

E

D

C

B

A

FAST Face Mask
© 2020
Mamma Can Do It

*All seam allowances
are included*
Cut 4

Cut on the fold

Fabric Grain

Size Chart

Size	Typical Age	Measure (page 3)
A	3-6 yr	up to 4"
B	6-10 yr	up to 4.5"
C	10-14	up to 5"
D	Adult	up to 5.5"
E	XL Adult	up to 6"

This page is intentionally blank

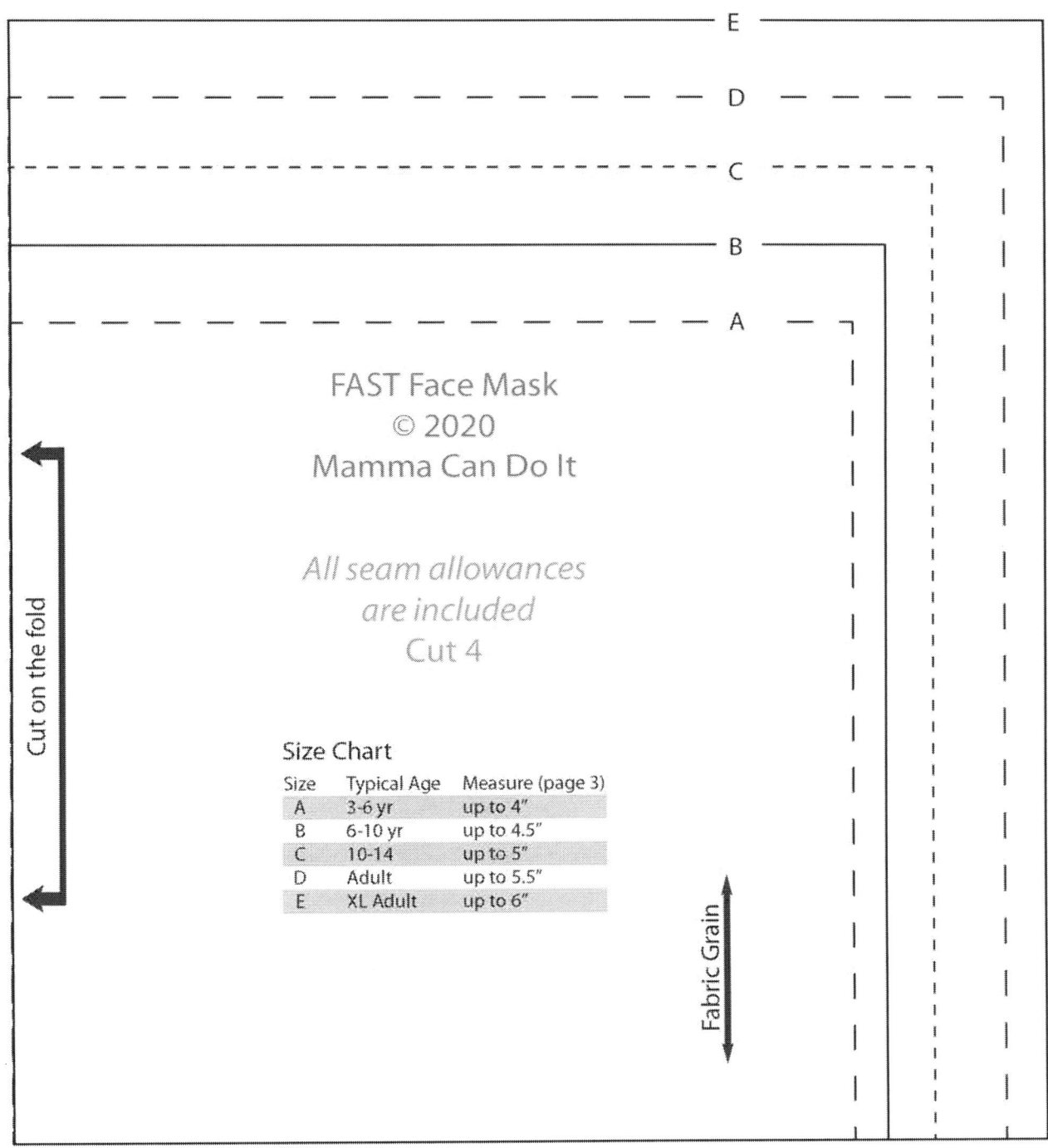

E

D

C

B

A

FAST Face Mask
© 2020
Mamma Can Do It

*All seam allowances
are included*
Cut 4

Cut on the fold

Fabric Grain

Size Chart

Size	Typical Age	Measure (page 3)
A	3-6 yr	up to 4"
B	6-10 yr	up to 4.5"
C	10-14	up to 5"
D	Adult	up to 5.5"
E	XL Adult	up to 6"

This page is intentionally blank

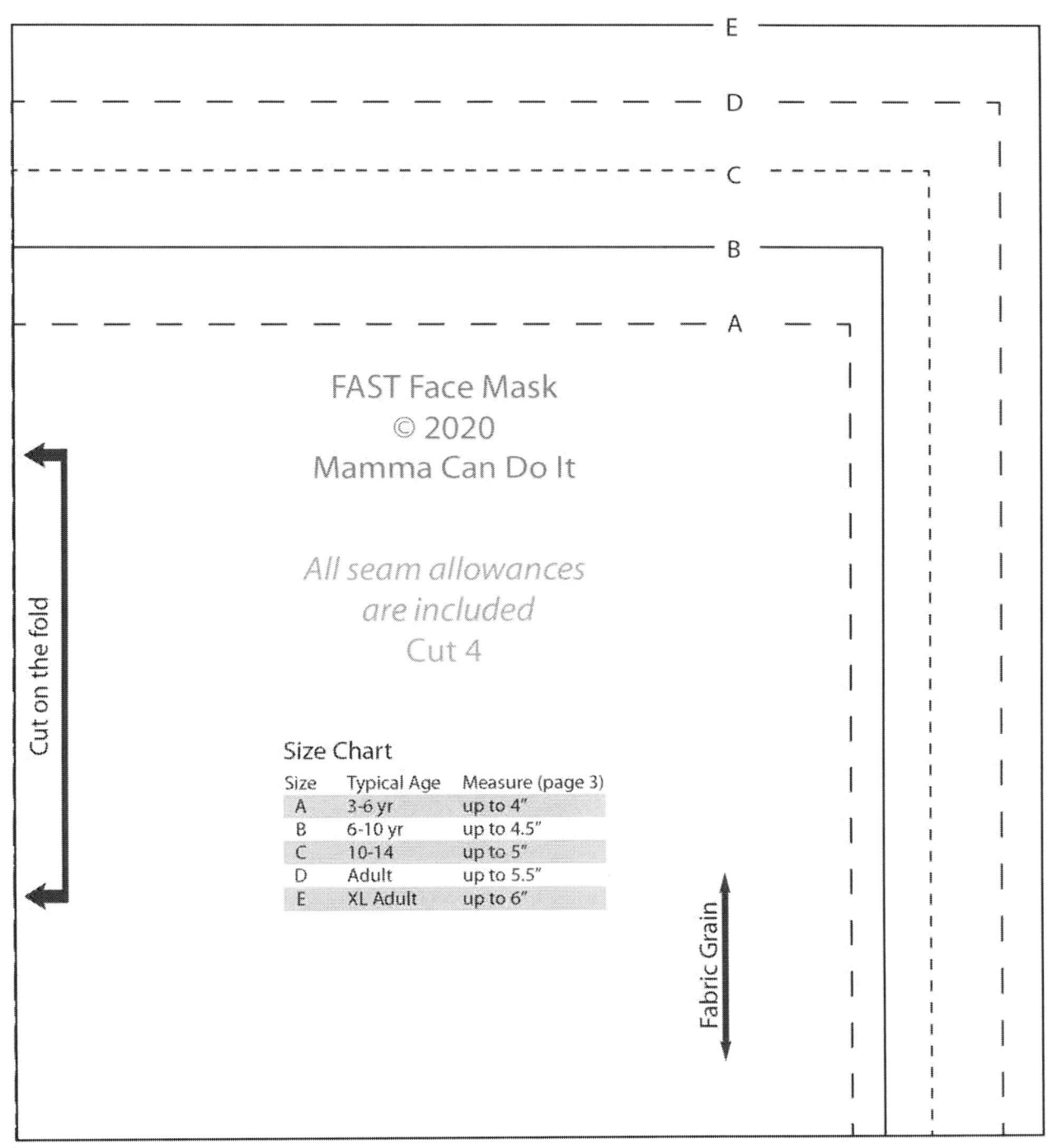

E
D
C
B
A

FAST Face Mask
© 2020
Mamma Can Do It

*All seam allowances
are included*
Cut 4

Cut on the fold

Fabric Grain

Size Chart

Size	Typical Age	Measure (page 3)
A	3-6 yr	up to 4"
B	6-10 yr	up to 4.5"
C	10-14	up to 5"
D	Adult	up to 5.5"
E	XL Adult	up to 6"

This page is intentionally blank

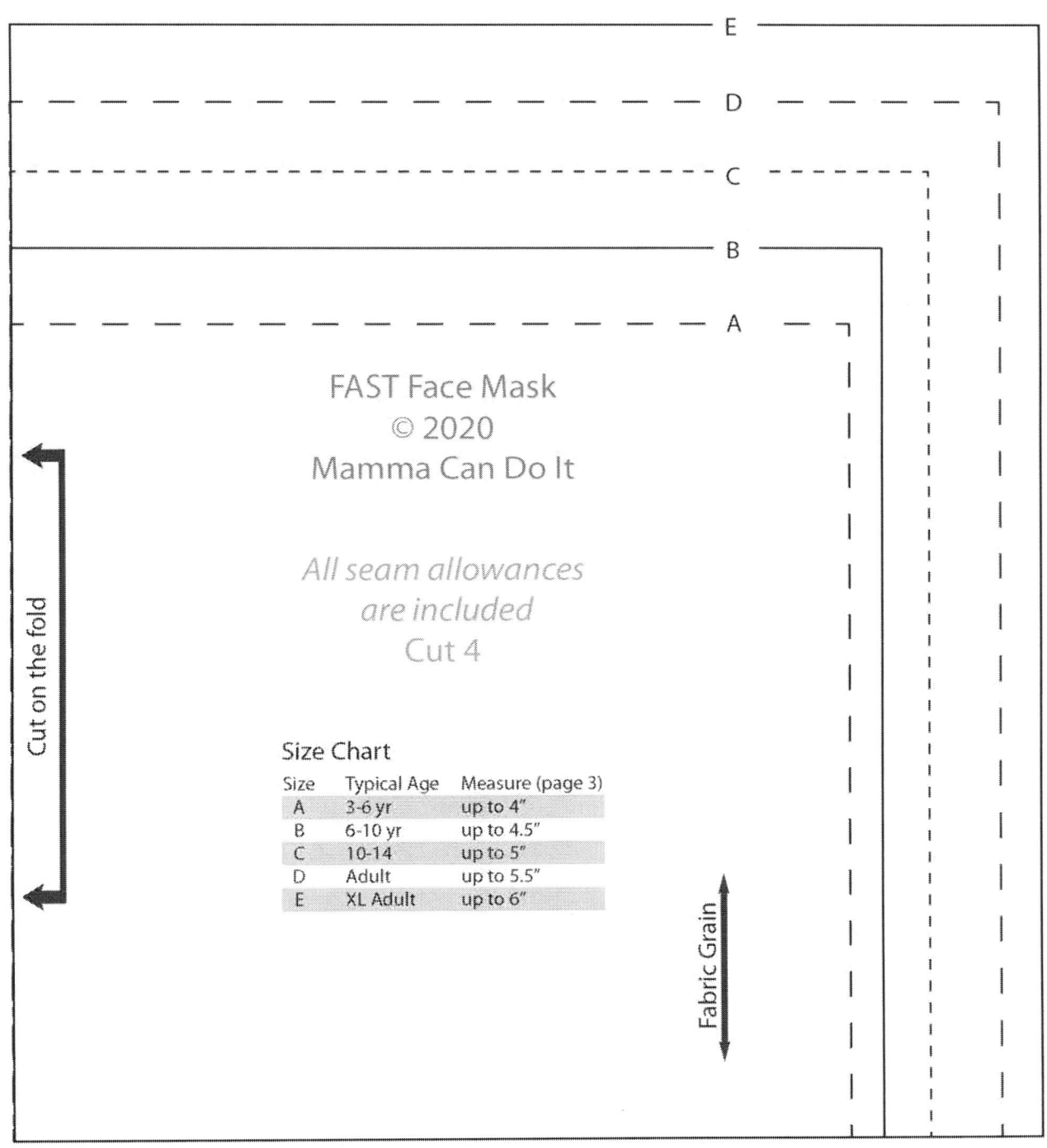

E

D

C

B

A

FAST Face Mask
© 2020
Mamma Can Do It

*All seam allowances
are included*
Cut 4

Cut on the fold

Fabric Grain

Size Chart

Size	Typical Age	Measure (page 3)
A	3-6 yr	up to 4"
B	6-10 yr	up to 4.5"
C	10-14	up to 5"
D	Adult	up to 5.5"
E	XL Adult	up to 6"

Manufactured by Amazon.ca
Bolton, ON